Bisquick Recipes To Tantalize Your Taste Bud: Bisquick Recipes For All Taste Buds

Ida Smith

Published by Ida Smith, 2021.

BISQUICK RECIPES TO TANTALIZE YOUR TASTE BUD: BISQUICK RECIPES FOR ALL TASTE BUDS

First edition. October 7, 2021.

ISBN: 979-8201304126

Written by Ida Smith.

Table of Contents

Introduction 1
Recipe 1 - Bisquick Fried dough 2
Recipe 2 - Crunchy Silky Bisquick Shortcake 4
Recipe 3 - Bisquick Double Chocolate Chips Chocolate Cookies 6
Recipe 4 - Bisquick Chocolate Coconutty Brownies 8
Recipe 5 - Bisquick Breakfast Flatbread 10
Recipe 6 - Bisquick Cocoa Churros 12
Recipe 7 - Extra Spicy Peanut Butter Bisquick Snowball 14
Recipe 8 - Spicy Bisquick Fried Corn Dog 16
Recipe 9 - Cinnamon-Sugar Crusted Bisquick Donut 18
Recipe 10 - Crispy Coated Bisquick Pork Chops 20
Recipe 11 - Veggie Bisquick Quiche 22
Recipe 12 - Bisquick Beer Battered Shrimp 24
Recipe 13 - Quick and Easy Bisquick Chicken Pot Pie 26
Recipe 14 - Bisquick Fish and Potato Patties 28
Recipe 15 - Toasty Bisquick Mix Fruity Waffles 30
Recipe 16 - Bisquick Sausage and Cheesy Hash Browns 32
Recipe 17 - Bisquick Bakes Sausage balls 34
Recipe 18 - Bisquick Herby Cheesy Biscuits 36
Recipe 19 - Bisquick Nutty Banana Bread 38
Recipe 20 - Bisquick Nutty Drop Scones 40
Recipe 21 - Bisquick Chicken Dumplings 42
Recipe 22 - Bisquick Chocolate Chips Pancakes 44
Recipe 23 - Bell Peppers Topping Bisquick Pizza 46
Recipe 24 - Bisquick Fried Ice Cream Balls 48
Recipe 25 - Breakfast Bisquick Blueberry Muffins 50
Recipe 26 - Bisquick Crumbly Buttery Cornbread 52
Recipe 27 - Bisquick Veggies Mac N' Cheese 54
Recipe 28 - Bisquick Tempered Chicken Fingers 56
Recipe 29 - Beet Red Bisquick Funnel Cake 58
Recipe 30 - Bisquick Coated Fried Fish 60
Conclusion 62

Introduction

Whether you are baking or looking for a shortcut to dinner, Bisquick is a kitchen angel. They come in handy at confusing times, and you end up with hugs and kisses for delicious recipes that make you feel like a hero.

Enough talk, let's get started and Bisquick away!

Recipe 1 - Bisquick Fried dough

Fried dough is a staple in many cultures around the world, and these are just the best. The exterior is crunchy with a fluffy interior.

Cook time 30 minutes

Makes a lot

Ingredients

- 3.5 cups Bisquick mix
- ¼ cup sugar
- 1 teaspoon nutmeg
- 3 tablespoons melted butter
- 1 teaspoon baking powder
- 2 eggs
- 1 cup milk
- Salt to taste

- Oil for frying

Method
Mix the dry ingredients and then add the wet ingredients to make a pliable but soft dough
Allow it to rest for 7 minutes
Heat the oil and add a spoonful into it to fry
Serve as desired

Recipe 2 - Crunchy Silky Bisquick Shortcake

Are you having guests for dinner? It is time to show your dessert skills with this recipe to wow your guests.

Serves 6

Cook time 20 minutes

Baking Time 375F

Ingredients

- 2 cups strawberry compote
- 2 cups chopped strawberries
- 2.5 cups Bisquick
- 150ml milk full cream
- 2 tablespoons sugar
- 3 tablespoons unsalted butter

Method

Mix the butter, sugar, and milk in a bowl

Add the Bisquick and pour in a round 6-inch pan
Cook until the skewer comes out clean
While still hot, pour the strawberry compote and refrigerate
Add the strawberries and serve

Recipe 3 - Bisquick Double Chocolate Chips Chocolate Cookies

The more chocolate, the better; this is a go-to snack that will please anyone.

Cook time 12 minutes
Bake Temp 350F
Serves 6
Ingredients

- 2 cups Bisquick
- ½ cup butter
- ½ cup dark chocolate
- ½ cup semi-sweet chocolate chips
- 2/4 cup brown sugar
- 1 large egg

Method
Cream the butter and sugar until fluffy
Add the egg and whisk
Add the Bisquick and fold in the chips
Scoop spoonful on a lined baking tray and bake until edges are golden brown
Cool and serve

Recipe 4 - Bisquick Chocolate Coconutty Brownies

This recipe is incredibly light and does not take all your time in the kitchen, put together in minutes and enjoy sooner.

Makes 12 squares
Cook time 30 minutes
Baking time 350F
Ingredients

- 2 cups Bisquick
- 1 cup dark chocolate
- ½ cup white baking chocolate
- 1 teaspoon Dutch Cocoa powder
- 30ml butter
- 1 ½ cups condensed milk
- 1 3/4 cups chocolate syrup

- ½ cup coconut flakes
- 1 egg
- ¼ teaspoons sea salt

Method

Melt the butter and dark chocolate in the microwave

Stir in the condensed milk, chocolate syrup, and egg

Add the Bisquick, cocoa powder, and coconut flakes

Pour in a non-stick baking pan, swirl in the white chocolate chips and bake until a skewer comes out mushy

Sprinkle the salt over, allow it to cool down, and cut to serve

Recipe 5 - Bisquick Breakfast Flatbread

If you love flatbread and cannot remember the recipe, this is the easiest way to get it done.

Cook time 15 minutes

Makes 6 – 10

Ingredients

- 2 cups Bisquick
- 2 tablespoons sugar
- 3 tablespoons olive oil
- ½ cup milk

Method

Mix the ingredients to form the dough, if it needs extra liquid, simply add few drops of water

Allow it to rest for 2-5 minutes

Make into balls and roll as thin as family

Cook in a non-stick pan until puffy with brown patches

Serve

Recipe 6 - Bisquick Cocoa Churros

These Mexican snacks are loved by all, and now you can make them at home with a Bisquick mix.

Cook time 20 minutes

Serves 6

Ingredients

- Oil for frying
- ¼ cup of sugar divided
- 2 teaspoons cinnamon
- 2 cups Bisquick mix
- 1 cup or more hot water

Method

Mix the cinnamon with half the sugar and set it aside

In a mixing bowl with the sugar and gradually pour in hot water to form a smooth dough

Scoop the mix in a piping bag and squeeze into the oil using scissors to cut when the desired length is reached

Fry to golden brown and toss in the sugar + cinnamon mix

Recipe 7 - Extra Spicy Peanut Butter Bisquick Snowball

These are simple cookie ball for even those that dislike sugar.

Cook time 3 hours

Serves 6

Bake Time 325F

- ¼ cup crushed peppermint to powder
- ¼ cup crushed crystalline ginger powder
- 1 cup peanut butter
- 1.5 cups Bisquick Mix
- Salt
- 1 teaspoon vanilla
- 2 cups powdered sugar

Method

Pour the Bisquick mix on a baking tray and toast in the oven until slightly brown for 3 to 5 minutes

Cool and pour in a bowl, and then add the remaining ingredients except for the powdered sugar

Make into dough and roll into balls

Throw the balls into the powdered sugar and enjoy

Recipe 8 - Spicy Bisquick Fried Corn Dog

Take your favorite sausage up a notch with this recipe; it is easy and will be ready in minutes for snack time.

Cook time 20 minutes

Serves 6

Ingredients

- Oil for frying
- 12 skewers soaked in water
- 1 packet of sausage containing 12 sausages
- ¾ cup Bisquick mix
- 1 tablespoon sugar
- ½ cup + 2 tablespoons milk
- ½ tablespoons ginger
- ¼ paprika smoked

Method

Heat the oil to 375F

Beat the egg and milk in a bowl with the ginger

Gradually fold in the Bisquick mix and sugar to form a thick batter

Insert the skewers into the hot dogs

Dip it into the batter and into the oil to fry

Serve

Recipe 9 - Cinnamon-Sugar Crusted Bisquick Donut

We all love sugar, and a touch of cinnamon is just perfect in elevating these donuts.

Cook time 70 minutes

Serves 4

Ingredients

- ½ teaspoons instant dry yeast
- 1 cup Bisquick mix
- 1 tablespoon sugar
- ½ cup milk warm
- ¼ cup sugar + 1 teaspoon cinnamon mixed
- 3 tablespoons butter
- Oil to fry

Method

Add the yeast in the milk and sugar for 5 minutes

Fold in the Bisquick mix, butter to make a dough, and allow to rest for 15 minutes

Knead and roll out to 1 inch thick

Cut with a donut cutter

Fry until golden brown and toss in cinnamon sugar

Recipe 10 - Crispy Coated Bisquick Pork Chops

What could be better than juicy pork chops coated in Bisquick for the crunch of a lifetime?

Serves 4

Cook time 50 minutes

Ingredients

- 1 tablespoon brown sugar
- 1 tablespoon paprika
- 1 teaspoon chili pepper
- 1 teaspoon garlic powder
- 1 teaspoon ginger
- ½ cup Bisquick
- 1/3 cup panko
- 1 egg

- Salt and pepper
- 4 pork chops about ½ inches thick
- 2 tablespoons milk
- ¼ cup butter

Method

Mix the brown sugar, paprika, chili pepper, garlic, and ginger, salt & pepper
Coat the pork chop and allow it to sit for 10 minutes
Meanwhile, mix the Bisquick with panko, season, and set aside
Mix the eggs with the milk and set aside
Dip the pork chops in the egg and then into the crumbs
Add the butter to the pan, fry the chops on low-med heat until brown
Doneness is according to your desire

Recipe 11 - Veggie Bisquick Quiche

This very simple and delicious recipe can be enjoyed any time of the day, just choose a comfortable spot, and savor it.

Cook time 40 minutes

Bake Time 400F

Serves 6

Ingredients

- 1 cup bacon crumbles
- 1.25 cups shredded Swiss cheese
- ¼ cup sweet onion
- 1 stalk of leeks chopped
- 1 teaspoon garlic minced
- 1 cup cauliflower
- 1 cup diced potatoes, parboiled

- 2 cups milk
- 1.25 cups Bisquick
- 4 large eggs
- Salt and pepper to taste

Method

Preheat the oven
Mix the cheese, bacon, onion, garlic, potatoes, leeks, cauliflower in a bowl
Pour in a bowl
Mix the Bisquick, milk, eggs, and seasoning
Pour over the veggies mix
Bake until brown, allow it to cool before serving

Recipe 12 - Bisquick Beer Battered Shrimp

Beer, shrimps, fried could not taste any better. This is simple, and you will be done in minutes, ready to enjoy with a bottle of your favorite beer brand.

Cook time 20 minutes

Serves 4

Ingredients

- 16 pieces of jumbo shrimps, peeled, deveined, and cleaned
- 2 cups of beer
- ¾ cup Bisquick mix
- 1 teaspoon garlic powder
- ½ teaspoons chili powder
- Salt and pepper
- 1 egg white

Method

Mix the eggs, beer, and Bisquick mix to form a light tempura-like batter
Season the shrimps with the spices and heat the oil, ready to fry
Dip the shrimps by the tail into the batter
Drop into the oil and remove when golden
Serve

Recipe 13 - Quick and Easy Bisquick Chicken Pot Pie

What could be better than chicken pot pie on cold and tiring evenings? Nothing, and this recipe is a keeper.

Cook time 50 minutes
Bake Temp 400F
Serve 6
Ingredients

- 2 cups canned chicken soup
- 3 cups mix veggies fresh or frozen
- 2 cups chicken pieces cooked
- 120ml milk
- 1 egg
- 1.5 cups Bisquick mix

- Salt and pepper

Method

Preheat the oven
Mix the chicken soup, veggie mix, and chicken cubes in a bowl and season
Pour in a baking dish, and then mix the rest (Bisquick, eggs, and milk)
Gentle pour over the chicken mix
Bake until golden brown and serve

Recipe 14 - Bisquick Fish and Potato Patties

Served with delicious tomato sauce for breakfast or dinner, this is a tasty recipe for everyone, including kids. After all, it saves you time from making fish and chips.

Cook time 30 minutes

Serves 6

Ingredients

- 4 cups diced parboiled Russet Potatoes
- 5 cups white steamed fish, flaked, no skin, and no bones
- 1 teaspoon garlic minced
- 1 red chili chopped
- 2 tablespoons scallion chopped
- 1 teaspoon paprika
- ½ cup – ¾ cup Bisquick mix

- 1 egg white
- Salt and pepper
- Oil for shallow frying

Method

Add all the ingredients in a bowl except the oil

Add the Bisquick quantity you need, if you like the floury taste, add more, but it is to bind it

Make the mix into patties and place in the pan on med heat

Fry until brown and flip to cook the opposite side

Serve

Recipe 15 - Toasty Bisquick Mix Fruity Waffles

Kids running late for school; whip up this easy batter and feed those little mouths

Cook time 15 minutes

Serves 4

Ingredients

- 2 cups Betty Crocker Bisquick mix
- 2 tablespoons melted butter
- 1 large egg
- 340ml milk
- 1 cup chopped fresh strawberries
- 1 cup whipped cream

Method

Mix the eggs, milk, and Bisquick to form a batter
Heat the waffle pan, brush with butter, and pour the batter on it
Cover and allow it to cook until brown
Repeat and serve with cream and fruits

Recipe 16 - Bisquick Sausage and Cheesy Hash Browns

Breakfast casseroles are life-savings recipes for large families. They are easy and versatile too.

Cook time 40 minutes

Bake Temp 450F

Serve 6 - 8

Ingredients

- 3 cups diced ham
- 3 cups breakfast sausage crumbled
- 2 cups milk
- 1 small white onion chopped
- 2 leek stalks chopped
- 6 eggs
- 2.5 cups cheddar cheese

- 1 ¾ cups Bisquick mix
- ½ teaspoons chopped red chili
- Salt and pepper to taste

Method

Add the sausage to a pan with the onion, leeks, and red chili until it is brown (drain out any excess fat)

Whisk the eggs, milk, and seasoning and add the cheese into it

Next, add the sausage, ham, and Bisquick mix

It should be thick and lump-free

Pour into a baking dish and cook until a skewer comes out clean

Serve after resting

Recipe 17 - Bisquick Bakes Sausage balls

Are you going tailgating or hosting your friends for a movie night? These are the perfect recipe to make your day bright and taste buds bubble.

Bake Temp 350F

Cook Time 25 minutes

Makes 16 balls

Ingredients

- 3 cups Bisquick mix
- 350g pork ground
- 250 beef ground
- 4 cups cheddar cheese
- ¼ cup chopped parsley
- 1 teaspoon pepper flakes

Method
Mix all the ingredients in a bowl
Make into balls
Arrange them on a tray and bake for 25 minutes
Serve with any dipping sauce

Recipe 18 - Bisquick Herby Cheesy Biscuits

Make tea time earthy and relaxing with these herby, cheesy biscuits that your guests will love it too.

Cook Time 15 minutes

Bake temp 450F

Make a lot

Ingredients

- 2 cups Bisquick mix
- 2/3 cup cream
- 1/3 cup + 2 tablespoons cheddar cheese
- 1.5 teaspoons fresh chopped basil
- 2 tablespoons unsalted butter
- Salt and black pepper
- Dash of garlic powder

Method

Mix the Bisquick, cream, cheese to form a soft dough
Stir in the basil and a dash of salt and pepper, and drop a spoonful on the baking tray
Mix the garlic and butter and gently brush over the biscuits
Sprinkle extra basil and bake until brown
Serve

Recipe 19 - Bisquick Nutty Banana Bread

Well, to avoid wasting overripe bananas, make this recipe with toasted nuts. It adds a crunch that calls for a second serving.

Cook time 70 minutes
Serves 6
Bake temp 350F
Ingredients

- 2 medium ripe or overripe bananas (about 2 cups)
- 1/3 cup white sugar
- 1/3 cup brown sugar
- 60ml milk
- 3 tablespoons melted butter
- 3 eggs

- 2 2/3 cups Bisquick mix
- ½ cup toasted nutmeg

Method

Whisk the eggs and the sugar in a bowl
Add the milk, milk, bananas and mix well
Fold in the Bisquick and pour into a loaf tin
Bake and allow it to cool down before slicing

Recipe 21 - Bisquick Chicken Dumplings

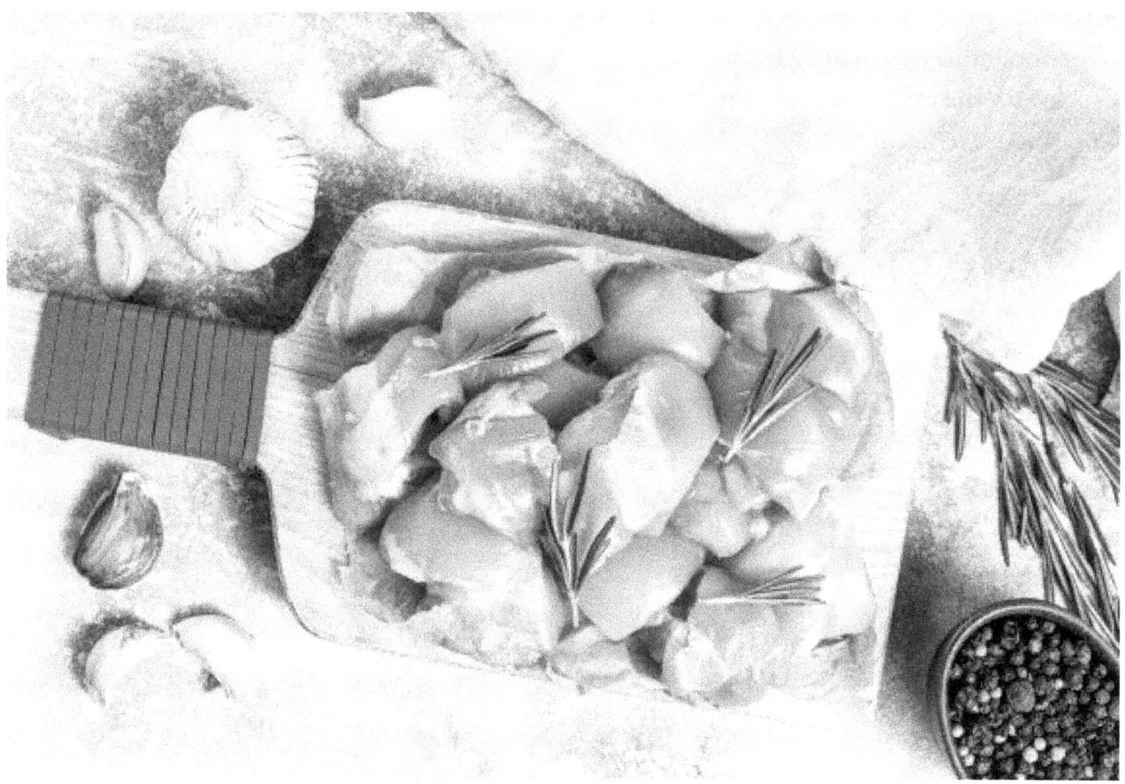

Fancy a bit of Chinese but cannot make it or call in, try these and sleep like a baby.

Cook time 50 minutes

Serves 4

Ingredients

- 6 chicken thighs boneless chopped to bits
- 1 cup celery chopped
- 2 large carrots diced
- 1 small onion diced
- 1 teaspoon garlic minced
- 4 cups chicken broth
- ¼ corn starch slurry
- 1 green pepper

- ½ cup frozen peas
- Salt and pepper
- 2 cups Bisquick mix
- 2/3 to ½ cup milk
- 2 tablespoons oil

Method

In a pan, sauté the onion, garlic, and celery until soft

Add the chicken piece, salt, and pepper, and allow it to cook

Meanwhile, make the dumpling by mixing the Bisquick with milk (gradually adding until the dough is formed)

Form into balls and refrigerate

Stir the chicken; add the carrots and broth to cook

Add the dumplings to cook for 1o minutes

Stir in the slurry, lower the heat, and then the peas

Serve

Recipe 23 - Bell Peppers Topping Bisquick Pizza

This is about the easiest pizza you will ever make, and it is delicious.

Oven Temp 450F

Cook time 10 minutes

Serves 4-6

Ingredients

- 2 bell peppers of all colors – red, yellow, and green, thinly sliced
- 1 large white sweet onion thinly sliced
- 14 cubes of mozzarella balls
- ½ cup chopped parsley
- Salt and pepper
- 2 cups tomato sauce
- 6 portabella mushrooms, thinly sliced

- ½ cup wheat flour
- 2 cups Bisquick mix
- 2 tablespoons olive oil
- 1 cup or more of water

Method

To make the pizza Bisquick dough, in a bowl, add the Bisquick mix, flour, olive oil, and then gradually add water to form a dough

Knead and rest for 10 minutes

Roll out the dough to a 10-inch round, spread the sauce,

Add the mozzarella all over, scatter the rest of the ingredients except the parsley

Sprinkle with salt and pepper and back until crisp

Sprinkle the parsley and a drizzle of olive oil

Serve

Recipe 24 - Bisquick Fried Ice Cream Balls

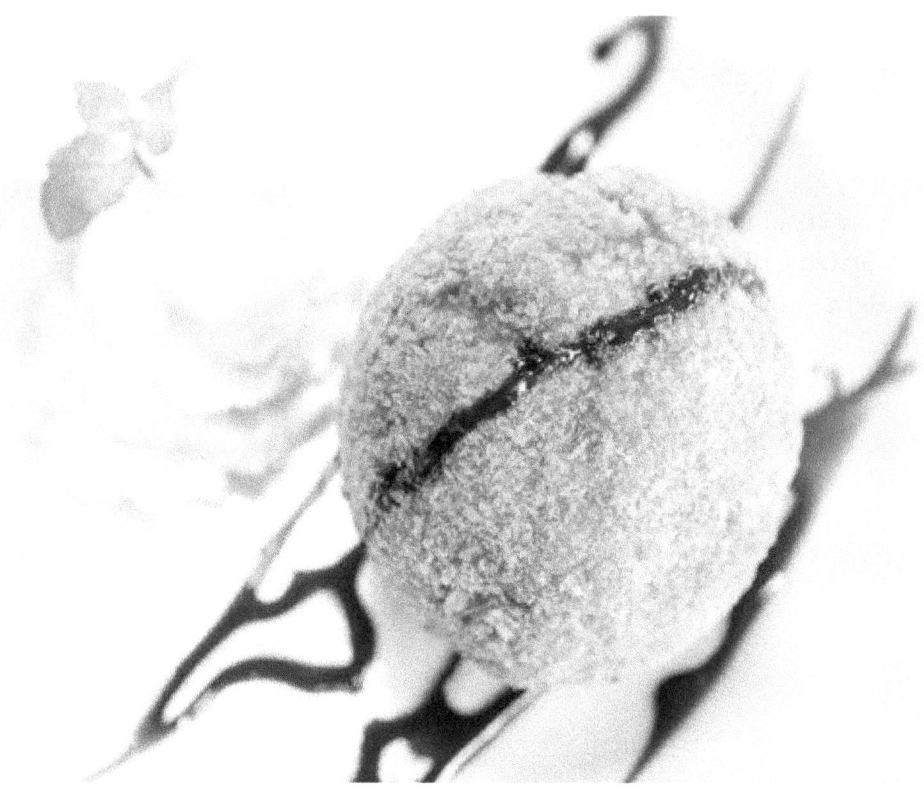

Crunchy ice cream and Bisquick; wow, but it does taste good. The recipe is as normal, just add Bisquick in there somehow.

Make time 20 minutes

Serves 6

Ingredients

- 6 large scoops of vanilla ice cream ball, frozen
- 1/3 cup Bisquick
- 3 cups rice puff cereal
- ½ teaspoons sea salt
- 2 cups sweetened whipped cream
- ½ teaspoons cinnamon
- 1 tablespoon butter

Method

Crumble the rice puffs and Bisquick with cinnamon in a deep bowl

Melt the butter and sauté the Bisquick mix until golden brown, season with the salt

Allow it to get cool and pour into a bowl

Take the frozen ice cream ball and quickly coat them in the cereal mix well

Refrigerate until you are ready to serve

Recipe 25 - Breakfast Bisquick Blueberry Muffins

What a delicious way to start breakfast than with fresh blueberries oozing out from the crumbled top?

Makes 12 muffins

Bake time 25 minutes

Bake Temp 400F

Ingredients

- 1 cup fresh blueberries
- 1 egg
- 2/3 cup almond milk
- ½ cup Bisquick
- 2 tablespoons butter
- 2 cups Bisquick mix
- ¼ cup brown sugar packed
- 2 tablespoons soy oil

Method

Preheat the oven and whisk the oil and sugar until melted
Add the eggs and milk
Fold in the flour and blueberries
Scoop the batter into the paper cups
Mix the Bisquick and butter to form a crumb
Sprinkle on the muffins and bakes
Serve

Recipe 26 - Bisquick Crumbly Buttery Cornbread

Ah, if you live in the south, cornbread is stable, and Bisquick just eased the preparation method.

Bake temp 350F

Cook time 40 minutes

Serves 8

Ingredients

- 2 cups Bisquick
- 1/3 cup yellow cornmeal
- ½ cup melted unsalted margarine
- 2 large eggs beaten
- 1 cup full cream milk
- 1/3 cup sugar
- ½ cup Parmesan cheese

Method

In a bowl, mix the Bisquick, cornmeal, and sugar together

In another one, add the melted butter to the eggs and beat in the milk and cheese

Gradually, mix both bowls together, stirring gently

Pour in a baking dish and into a preheated oven until brown and cracking

Serve as desired

Recipe 27 - Bisquick Veggies Mac N' Cheese

We all love Mac N' cheese, with a little Bisquick topping, and it is heaven on a plate.

Cook time 55 minutes

Serves 6

Bake Temp 400F

Ingredients

- 2 cups parboiled elbow macaroni at least 3-5 minutes drained
- 3 cups freshly shredded cheddar
- 2 cups milk
- ¼ cup sour cream
- ½ teaspoons black pepper
- ½ teaspoons onion and garlic powder
- 3 eggs

- 4 -5 drops Tabasco sauce
- ¾ cup Bisquick mix

Method

Preheat the oven

Mix the Mac n cheese with the ingredients but keep aside ½ the cheese and Bisquick

Pour in a bowl

Mix the cheese with the Bisquick and sprinkle over the Mac n' cheese

Cover with a foil sheet, remove for the last 2 minutes to brown

Serve

Recipe 28 - Bisquick Tempered Chicken Fingers

Chicken with the extra crunch that Bisquick provides and a perfect dip is the perfect snack for anyone. This recipe is good as you want it to be.

Cook time 50 minutes

Serves 4

Ingredients

- 3 chicken breasts boneless/skinless cut in strips
- 1 teaspoon chili flakes
- 1 teaspoon curry powder
- 1 teaspoon cumin, ginger, and garlic powder
- 1 tablespoon sugar
- Salt and pepper
- ½ cup Bisquick

- 1 cup water
- 1 egg
- Oil to fry

Method

Add the spices in a bowl with the chicken strips and sugar, massage them together and allow it to sit for 15minutes

Meanwhile, beat the egg in a bowl and mix the Bisquick with water to form a light but adhesive batter

Wash the chicken pieces and dip them into the Bisquick batter

Quick throw them down gently into the oil and cook until golden brown and delicious

Serve with any dipping sauce of your choice

Recipe 29 - Beet Red Bisquick Funnel Cake

Enjoy a crunchier funnel cake using Bisquick; it is light and airy too.

Cook time 12 minutes

Serves 4

Ingredients

- 2 cups Bisquick Original
- 1 – 2 tablespoons beet juice concentrated
- 1 whole egg
- 1 egg white
- 1 cup full cream milk
- Oil for frying

Method

Whisk the egg and egg white with the milk and beet concentrate
Add the Bisquick mix until smooth
Pour the batter into a piping bag with a funnel tip
Pipe into hot oil, moving your hand in a circle
Fry until crisp
Serve

Recipe 30 - Bisquick Coated Fried Fish

It's Bisquick, and it works just fine here. It is extra crumbling too.

Serve 4

Cook time 8 -10 minutes

Ingredients

- 4 white fish fillets skinless, boneless
- ½ cup Italian crumbs
- ½ cup Bisquick
- 1 egg white beaten
- 1 teaspoon garlic powder
- Salt and pepper
- Oil for frying
- Lemon wedges for serving

Method
Season the fish fillets with salt and pepper
Mix the Bisquick, crumbs, garlic powder, salt, and pepper in a bowl
Dip the fish in the egg wash
Coat with the Bisquick mix
Fry until crisp
Serve with lemon wedges

Conclusion

Cooking is supposed to be fun, and Bisquick Mix is a great way to cook delicious recipes that will excite your taste buds. These recipes listed here are to pique your interest. Bisquick is a versatile ingredient, and your imagination is the limit.

Enjoy!

Don't miss out!

Visit the website below and you can sign up to receive emails whenever Ida Smith publishes a new book. There's no charge and no obligation.

https://books2read.com/r/B-A-LRXL-IOMSB

www.ingramcontent.com/pod-product-compliance
Ingram Content Group UK Ltd.
Pitfield, Milton Keynes, MK11 3LW, UK
UKHW061655190726
13853UKWH00008B/2218

9 798201 304126